# Useful Tips with "Links" for South Africa

# Useful Tips with "Links" for South Africa

Travel Guide with
Personal Experiences and Pictures:
Cape Town, Garden Route,
Pretoria, Kruger Park
(Easy to read)

@ 2014
Irmgard Hetterich

**Bibliografische Information der Deutschen Nationalbibliothek**
Die Deutsche Nationalbibliothek verzeichnet diese Publikation in der Deutschen
Nationalbibliografie; detaillierte bibliografische Daten sind im Internet über http://dnb.d-
nb.de abrufbar.

@ 2014 Irmgard Hetterich

Herstellung und Verlag:
BoD - Books on Demand
Norderstedt

ISBN: 978-3-7357-9081-1

# Inhalt

# My trip to South Africa

I took a short trip with my husband to South Africa in March 2012 because my son was staying there for some time to visit a friend. It was a good chance for us to fly there; we thought he would be able to help us. We waited until the hot weather was over. I think the country is such a beautiful place to visit. There are different kinds of vegetation, green areas, many different sorts of trees and botanical gardens, vineyards, scenic highlands, mountains, natural reserves, and animals as well as enormous gorgeous coasts. We took many pictures and I decided to write this travel guide for others, who are unfamiliar with this country.

We flew on March 16, 2012 from Germany to South Africa with South African Airlines. We did not want to change planes on the way, so we took a direct flight from Munich, Germany to Johannesburg, South Africa. That flight takes 11 hours, and it depends from where you fly, but if possible, *try not to change planes because the waiting time will add to the flight time*. There are less expensive flights, but they usually take three to four hours more with the additional stop.

Here I found a lot of useful information for my trip. http://www.suedafrikaurlaub.net/, but if you don't speak German you can look at http://www.southafrica.com/

Someone told me the next address is good for everything one ever needs to know about anywhere:
http://www.tripadvicer.com/
But I feel a lot of information does not help others as much as personal experiences, as I have written here for the readers.

You sit all those hours in a tight seat. Either the seats in airplanes are getting smaller or I'm getting fatter. OK. I gained weight since our last flight over 10 years ago, but I heard the seats are getting smaller. We left at about 9 P.M. so that we could sleep on the way. Did I say something about sleeping? That was impossible. If I had enough money to fly business class, I'm sure the seats would have been more comfortable and I would have been able to fall asleep.

You are not allowed to lie on the floor of the plane, but that is what I would have liked to do. My husband was sitting next to me by the window, and his back hurt. My backside hurt, and it was so uncomfortable. They had ear plugs to listen to music or see a film. My husband knew how to use the screen in front of us, but I was having difficulty. He found a film in German, but I wanted to watch one in English. I used to live in New York and went to school there, so I can understand the language well. I also teach English in evening courses in Germany.

By the time my equipment finally functioned it was already late. I watched the film "Transformers," but just a short version, and afterwards I did not want to start another one. It was too difficult to get one going, so I gave up. (The problem may be that I was too impatient and pushed too many buttons, because it took so long until something showed up on the screen.)

On the morning of March 17, 2012, we landed in Johannesburg and walked through the airport. Someone asked my husband something and even though I did not hear him, I knew what he wanted. I said my husband doesn't speak English and we do not need a taxi. Outside at least three taxi drivers were hoping to get us to ride with them, but I repeated that my son is picking us up. We had not waited long when he arrived. Our two big suitcases didn't fit in the trunk, so one had to be placed next to me on the back seat. *My son told us never to leave any bags or things on the back seat because someone could break through the window and take it even while you are in the car.* That sounds dangerous, I thought. *When you leave the car, everything must be placed into the trunk.* So we listened to our son and always packed everything up when leaving the car.

9

I had also read on the Internet some advice about what you should not do in South Africa if you don't want to be recognized as a tourist. I had planned to use a fanny pack to carry important things with me. That was something one should not do, according to these security rules. *This is apparently a sign for thieves that you have a lot of money with you, and they cut the bag from your body.* After reading this, I decided to take a backpack.

At home I spent weeks on the Internet to find out about things to see and accommodations in South Africa. I searched for German B&Bs, because I am German, but of course they also speak English. I booked them in advance so that we would not have to look for any accommodations while on route. *In South Africa I saw some Information Centers like we have in Germany, but not all over, so it is better if you know in advance where you will spend the night.* Some places were inexpensive, and with some I asked for a reduction in price since it was off-season and they still had availability. I did that all the time and was able to save some money (about 50 Euros). If you do not go to South Africa in the summer, which is in December, January and February, you will find vacant rooms all over. I heard you can find easily places to sleep without having to book in advance and you can haggle the price down, but then you don't know what you are going to get. If you have seen the pictures in the Internet in advance you will have some idea, but there are not always pictures, and some can be misleading.

It took an hour from the airport in Johannesburg to North Pretoria. After a short rest in the afternoon, we drove around a bit. We went to the Voortrekker Monument where we had a good view of the area.

http://www.voortrekkermon.org.za


It was very windy up there. Then we visited the Parliament Building, where they had a striking huge green park with colorful flowers. There was a bride with guests drinking champagne and taking pictures. It was such a gorgeous, sunny day, and with the beautiful scenery all around, they had chosen a good place for their pictures. We bought some wooden figures at vendors on the sidewalk opposite the building. In South Africa you can find such vendors selling souvenirs on the streets and other places those tourists frequent.

Before flying to Cape Town we stayed a couple of days in North Pretoria with our son. He was spending some time there and booked the flights for us from Johannesburg to Cape Town and back from Port Elisabeth. It was his idea to drive only one way, so we had to find a car rental that would also accommodate this wish. It cost us a little extra, but we saved time. He booked a small hut for us where he was staying in "Thabela Afrika – The guesthouse for the discerning businessman and holiday maker" in Akasia, Pretoria. http://www.thabela.co.za

The woman who owns this huge, secure estate, which is surrounded by electrical fences, has lived in South Africa for 45 years. She is German and reminded me of my aunt because she looked like her. She also has two sons like I do, and both are in Germany. During my visit I met Germans who left Germany to start a new live in South Africa. I found out that you have to bring 150.000 Euros with you in order to start a business there. I suppose some people believe they can have a better life in a foreign country, whatever purpose they might have to leave Germany or another country. I would not want to leave Germany in order to live in South Africa, because I enjoy the freedom and security in my country. But South Africa certainly also has many opportunities for a good life.

What we noticed right at the beginning is that walls or fences surrounded all the houses and properties.

Whenever we needed help along the way there were friendly security men in yellow vests. I remained in areas where tourists visit and generally felt very safe. I didn't go to any of the poor housing areas or walk around in any city areas without any security personnel.

## Huge fruits and vegetables

On the way to our "home" we stopped at a supermarket so that we could grill in the evening. I had never seen so many fruits and vegetables in one place, and they were all so enormous! It seemed to me as if I was in a future film, because all the food was so gigantic. Did they have some kind of secret on how to grow everything bigger than anywhere in the world? I never saw such huge onions, fruits, and vegetables before. Perhaps they are treated with radiation, as in the film "Godzilla."

There was such a huge choice of meat, and one sausage--I had to take a picture--must have been 10 meters long! I was amazed.

The most important thing for me is water. I have to drink a lot, and there were these huge plastic canisters of water, perhaps 5 gallons in size. In March it is not so hot, but in February I heard it was very hot and can be up to over 40 degrees Celsius there.

Many also sell fruits and vegetables on the road. At traffic lights in the city they come up to your car with grapes, water, or newspapers. My son said we should *always raise our hands friendly and say "no thanks"*. Some go around with plastic bags to collect your garbage in the car. One time I was thinking of giving one my empty plastic water bottles to a man, but then the light had already turned green. I suppose then you also have to give them some money and not just the empty bottles, which are thrown away.

# Friendly People

I must mention that all the people that I met during my trip in South Africa were very friendly. In the supermarkets young girls at the checkout all smiled and were friendly. All were curious about where we were from. I usually explained that we were from Germany and talked to them a little bit. I told them where we are staying and where we are going. I did the same with all the men at the parking lots and found out some interesting things about them or the area. For example one told me he prefers to work in the evening because he does not like the heat in the day.

Even in the bathrooms I often talked to the cleaning women, who were always very friendly. Every time you meet someone in South Africa, they say "hello, how are you?" and, as *I learned from my son, you should always respond with "fine thanks, and you"?* It doesn't matter if you are not feeling good. This question is always meant as a greeting and not meant to solicit complaints about all your illnesses.

It is also expected that you look each other in the eyes when you greet them. What you are saying is, "I recognize you as a person and am glad that you are concerned about my well being."

# Rhino & Lions Park

On Sunday we visited the "Rhino and Lions" Park near Johannesburg. We saw many animals, and the weather was perfect. Actually, we had such luck with the weather the whole time we were in South Africa. It was warm, not too hot, and mostly sunny. Now and then it was cloudy, but that was good for driving, and it prevented us from getting sun burnt.

At the entrance of the park, they give you a schedule so you know when the animals come out to be fed. I thought the man on the open truck who threw the raw meat down to the lions had a dangerous job. What would have happened if the lions or the leopards had decided to eat him instead? One animal even had his two front paws on the back of the truck as the man was throwing the meat down!

My son, husband and I had our cameras and took many pictures. Across the street, on the other side of the entrance, many lions and tigers roamed behind fences. I took some good pictures of them because they were so close, but securely behind fences. The hippopotamuses were also on land in the evenings. Normally you only see the two eyes looking out of the water when they are not. These animals can be very dangerous.

On the way home, we went to "Carnivore," a very famous restaurant outside of Johannesburg with about 1000 seats. It is enormous. http://carnivore.co.za./ui/multi/onepager/prm

Naturally, our car was very dirty from driving through the red sand in the park, and the man watching the cars at the parking lot offered to clean ours for 50 Rands. That was a good deal, so we went for it. Because it was off season, there were not too many people, and we were able to sit outside.

At the restaurant you pay one price and eat as much grilled meat and side dishes as you want. The waiter comes around with different types of meat-- zebra, kudu, crocodile, lamb, beef, chicken and pork--and cuts off the pieces you want to eat. It comes with different dips, some rice and backed potatoes. (More rice then potatoes, which I preferred. You need to ask for more of them.) *Avoid the edge of the meat that is very black or the inside that is still raw. Tell them exactly how you like it cooked.* My son had digestive problems that night, probably the result of eating too much of the charred meat. But in general the food in South Africa was very good and inexpensive, even if it sometimes seemed to wage war against my digestive system.

We did not have enough cash, so my son tried to pay with his South African credit card. It took a long time to pay because some of the credit card machines did not function correctly and/or the waiters

17

did not know how to operate them. We were afraid we might have to wash dishes if they could not get the machine to work, but in the end, it (thankfully) functioned.

# Merchants and tents

On Monday, we visited the fair. We drove a long time on a straight road and saw walls and fences surrounding houses, estates with beautiful trees and green land. We noticed that in South Africa many roads are very straight and in good condition. There was probably much repaving done because they hosted the world soccer games a few years ago. Sometimes we would see black people walking along these long roads, and I wondered where they are going. There were no buildings for miles, meaning they would have to walk for hours to reach anything.

After an hour, we reached a huge tent filled with wooden carved animals and other small souvenirs. We bought a few things and went further to the next big tent. Five merchants surrounded us immediately by the entrance trying to sell us their goods. My husband was looking for a cap. After we described what my husband was looking for, one of the vendors came back with it. . After that, each merchant wanted us to buy something from them. You could not walk around and look without someone showing you something that you should buy. In the high season there are enough customers to keep them all satisfied, but on the off-season, they all want to sell something to you.

I mentioned that I was interested in a small, light brown elephant, and several merchants ran around and showed me, what he found. One of the small elephants was perfect, and I paid 30 Rands. My husband thought that was too expensive. However, I had already haggled him down from 60 to 30 Rands, so I felt satisfied. *You always have to negotiate with the sellers.*

After an hour of shopping, I said that this is too much for me because it is always so hard for me to say "no". I talked with many of the merchants, and my husband constantly had to wait for me. Everyone asked where we were from and, after I told them we were German, they said "Germany good." (They probably meant "good for business.") In the end, I was glad to leave the fair, and when we came to another in Cape Town, I did not even go in. I was just too exhausted.

Cape Town

We planned to take a short trip of nine days to see the "Garden Route," which starts in Mossel Bay and goes to Port Elizabeth. This famous tourist area is on the south and east coast of South Africa and has its name because it is like a big garden with lots of trees, huge natural reserves, and beautiful coasts.

We flew to Cape Town on a cheap airline booked by our son. We do not fly very often, but each time we have flown, we got something to eat and to drink on the plane. That is what I expected this time too. But the stewardess told me we have to pay if we want any food. What? We have to pay? Apparently, since this is a cheap flight, food and drinks are not included. Oh, I was surprised. What have you got? Sandwiches? No thanks. We can wait to eat in the evening in a nice restaurant.

In Germany we had booked a car with a GPS system so that we could quickly find all locations without having to look at a map. Only my husband and I would be taking the trip to the Garden Route because my son was taking an excursion with his friends to Botswana with a rented car. They drove over 1000 km there and back again in four days! That is something young people can endure but not such "old" ones like me and my husband.

We had nine days to drive 800 km from Cape Town to Port Elisabeth. But I can tell you now that nine days is not enough. *You should take your time to travel this lovely area and two weeks should be the minimum.* This beautiful area was a recommendation from Herbert's Uncle, who said we have to visit the "Garden Route" when we fly to South Africa. He and his wife have already been there and were certain we would love it. That was the best thing we did on the trip, and we are so glad we followed his advice.

In South Africa they drive on the left side of the street as they do in England, and my husband had a little difficulty remembering that. I helped him by periodically telling him he needed to drive to the left because the cars are coming our way. When turning right I always said "drive over there on your left". "Why do you look to your right? You've got to look to your left before driving right"! It is not so easy to change your habit of looking to the right if a car is coming, but you must learn quickly, since they are all coming from the other direction.

We had a GPS in the car but made a mistake. We told the car rental we wanted to go to a road in Cape Town, and the women at the airport put it on the navigation for us. But actually, we were staying in a suburb called Oranjezicht and not in the city center. We drove at first through the wrong streets. The whole way seemed wrong because I had seen pictures on the Internet of "The Blue Sky Hotel", our B&B, and it was on a hill overlooking Cape Town with a beautiful view of the city lights at night. http://www.bluesky-bb.co.za/index.htm

To find our hotel, we had to change the town name, although it was a part of the city. I'm glad that I wrote the name down. The same mistake almost happened another time in Port Elisabeth, but then I remembered that *the suburb name has to be written instead of the city name.*

I had picked out all our sleeping accommodations at home in Germany on the Internet and wrote them down in my calendar, so that I would know where we had to go each day. It is also important to look at the size of the bed when you are as tall as my husband and I. Some beds are not too big. A King- size or Queen- size bed is ideal.

I chose only German B&Bs because many wanted an advanced payment, and if you pay with the "Rand" -the money from South Africa, - then you have to pay more for the transaction at the bank. Most of the German B&Bs had an account at a bank in Germany. With some, we did not need to pay anything in advance and just paid upon departure. It naturally depends on which country you come from, but there probably are people from your country who have moved to South Africa. Many have opened a B&B or hotel and speak multiple languages, especially English.

The owner gave us a city map and recommended we eat at the harbor called "Waterfront," which is a huge tourist attraction. Many different nationalities were present and you could hear different languages. Naturally, most speak English. It was not so easy to decide where to eat. There were so many by the water. We ate fish at a nice restaurant on the balcony (can't remember the name) and afterwards walked around a huge shopping mall directly on the harbor.

The best way to see the city and learn a lot about the area is to take a sightseeing bus, which we did. They have audio systems that allow you to choose from many languages.

http://www.citysightseeing.co.za/

The next day we took a sightseeing bus in order to see as much as possible. We drove down the hill to bus stop number 7, as was suggested, and I saw the Mount Nelson Hotel nearby. There were huge round white stone pillars at the entrance. We had planned to take the red bus for a city tour, but the blue bus arrived first. We did not want to wait any longer and decided to take the bigger tour that also drives into the countryside and had additional stops at a botanical garden, a bird sanctuary and vineyards. We did not know that you have to pay in advance for two days, but we figured we would have a few hours the following day. This ticket also includes a sunset evening tour to Signal Hill and a half hour boat ride on the canal.

We sat upstairs in the open area because we had good weather and wanted to take some pictures. My husband and I have a digital camera, and we took many pictures! (All together 500 and 400) We stayed on the bus until we got to Haut Bay, a fishing-village with small boats and a white sand beach with some tourists. How cold is the water? I did not test it personally, but heard later that the ocean around Cape Town is too cold to swim without wetsuits. We walked along to the boats and saw some seals being fed. With the two day ticket you can take the red or the blue bus. From here the red bus drove along the coast and through the city. We drove into the city passing by beautiful beaches on the left and huge mountains on the right side.

Once we got out of the bus at the number 4 bus stop, I looked at the map. There was something about a round trip walking tour noted on the city map. A security man came over to me, and I told him we plan to go to the number 10 bus stop by foot. All over the city where tourists walk around, they had special security workers wearing yellow vests and carrying a baton in their pocket. We did not see many police officers, but security people were everywhere to protect the visitors of the city. He showed me the designated route on the city map for the city walking tour and said we should walk around only in the local area. The trip to the number 10 bus stop is too far away and too dangerous.

We decided to listen to him and not take any unnecessary chances. *My son said you have to watch out in the city for your belongings and not take too much money.* I noticed many people pay with a credit card everywhere so that they did not need to carry too much money around. *In some supermarkets they even had a problem changing large bills, so it is better to take change and smaller bills with you when traveling.* On the other hand, sometimes the ATM machines did not always function at some of the places we were.

I asked why there were so many people on the road, and someone told me that March 21 is the day of freedom and a holiday in South Africa. We walked to the entrance of the park, where many black people were spending the holiday with family. We did not have too much time because we wanted to catch the next bus and therefore we did not see too much of the park. My husband saw a squirrel and took a picture of it. In Germany we don't have too many squirrels, but I know they do in America. I used to live there and saw them all the time. The park was near the St. George's Cathedral, (I'm not sure if that was the name), which was not open, so we decided to take the bus by the number 5 bus stop and not walk back around to the number 4, as was suggested on the map.

On this special city route designated for tourists there were many security guards to insure that none of the tourists was robbed or bothered by poor people begging for money.

We had also eaten on a road designated for tourists before the bus stop, and there was a thin hungry man who looked at the people sitting at the restaurant. I was about to give him a piece of my sandwich, but then a young man from another table gave him something to eat first.

In the afternoon we arrived at the Table Mountain, which is part of the Table Mountain National Park, which stretches from Signal Hill all the way to Cape Point. The Table Mountain National Park is part of the single richest floristic area in the world. It is a World Heritage Site with over 1460 different species of vegetation, including the King Protea, South Africa's national flower. You get up to the mountain in a cable car that turns around while ascending or descending. That was new to us.

We had heard that you have to wait a long time to go up there, but we were lucky. We got out of the bus in the afternoon and went directly into the cable car without having to wait. We spent about two hours up there enjoying the beautiful view of the city, mountains, and the ocean. We took a lot of lovely pictures, including of the Lion's Head Mountain, exotic birds, and small black lizards. You can also see Robben Island which used to be a prison for political prisoners like Nelson Mandela.

It was such a nice day and the sun was shining so much that we had to be careful not to get sunburned. Never go up a mountain without suntan lotion.

Then we returned to the Waterfront, where our evening bus tour started at 6 p.m. They say that at Signal Hill you can observe a beautiful sunset. *This trip is included with the blue bus ticket for the two day tour.* An employee recommended enjoying a picnic while watching the sunset, and we had enough time at the Waterfront to buy something to eat. We found the supermarket we had seen the night before in the big shopping center and bought bread, cheese, water and wine. That was a good idea, because I got hungry up there, and it was late when we drove down again. On the way up the sun was already setting over the ocean and reflected sensationally. We kept driving higher and higher and saw a lot.

Normally in the summer time the sun sets later but in March it got dark at about seven o'clock, so the tour was not as long as written on the brochure. We had a very long day in Cape Town and saw many things twice because the evening tour drove along the coast and up the hill. I asked the bus driver if he could let us out on the way back in the area where we parked the car. That was by bus stop number 7 near the Mount Nelson Hotel. He let us out at a corner and said we should walk two blocks straight ahead and then turn right.

We walked down the dark road and it got darker and darker. At the next crossroad my husband said we should turn left. Why? I think the bus driver said we should go straight and then turn right. We looked at the dark street ahead and were not so happy about going straight. There were no street lights. Luckily there was a parking attendant nearby with a yellow vest. When he saw us, he quickly crossed the street to help us because we probably looked like lost tourists. I said our car is around the corner from the Mount Nelson Hotel. He told us to turn around and go back to where a person was standing further down on the sidewalk and there we should go left. That was after the dark road that I thought we had to take. To our surprise we were at the Mount Nelson Hotel, but not at the entrance where the pillars are. It is a huge building complex, not just one building. I asked the soldier at the gate if we could walk through the hotel parking lot because our car is on the other side. Luckily I had noticed this building as we were waiting for the bus in the morning. My husband had no idea where our car was, but I did. After reaching the huge white pillars where there were also guards, I told my husband that our car was now around the corner. I always pay attention to where we park in case my husband forgets.

We had parked on a good street where all the houses have 24 hours alarm systems and security. There are signs on the entrances in English for 24 hour security, but my husband did not know what they meant. A security guard came to us, and I said we are happy that we found our car so that he would not think we were stealing it.

The next day we drove to the Cape of Good Hope, where we also had wonderful weather. We drove down along the Atlantic Ocean coast and had a beautiful view of the water and mountains. We stopped at a small parking area and another car came from the other direction. The driver drove back and forth many times before finally stopping. I said to my husband, this man cannot drive. But then an older couple got out; the man must have been about 80 years old. They both talked to me, and I found out that they used to live in South Africa many years ago. At that time there were many Europeans living here, especially from Italy. But the couple returned to London because their children moved there. They mentioned that many Europeans who used to live in South Africa have since returned to Europe. I found that very interesting. I wondered if they were talking about the "Apartheid" period or another time. Many years ago many blacks killed white people because the whites were rich and owned land and the native people were poor. I saw that on the news and read about it in Time Magazine. But those days are over and no one needs to be frightened because of his color.

You can spend a whole day on the Cape of Good Hope, but we did not have that much time. It was very beautiful all over. They have special trees that you do not see in Europe. We were lucky to have so much sun in the middle of March, which is the South African fall. The temperature was mostly 24 – 27 degrees Celsius.

Late in the afternoon we drove to Stellenbosch. On the way we stopped shortly before Simon's Town on Boulders Beach. There you can see many penguins that are smaller than those in the Arctic.

As I got out of the car, I noticed a park attendant there. I said politely "hello, how are you?" and he said "fine thanks and you?" I talked a short time to practically all the park attendants I met while we were driving around in South Africa. It made me feel happy when he answered my words "see you later" with "it will be a pleasure". I wanted to be friendly and convey that I accept him as a person and will treat him with respect.

We paid our entrance fee and walked along a boardwalk. My husband was skeptical that there would be any penguins there. But soon we came to some people who were looking over the railing and taking pictures. My husband also took out his camera and started taking pictures. The funny thing was that all the tourists were taking pictures of this one penguin, when just around the corner there were so many more! Many penguins were sitting on the rocks and lying on the beach. Some penguins jumped out of the water, while others were lying on their babies, which you could see when they moved a little bit. It was terrific! They actually do have penguins here and so many of them!

We took many pictures, and although the sun was shining, it was getting cold because of the wind. On the way back to the exit we saw the new visitors taking pictures of the first penguin near the entrance. Knowing now what they did not know yet, we had to laugh. Everyone gets excited to see their first penguin, and they all take a picture of him. Then they go around the corner and are surprised to see many more penguins on the beach.

I had my 3 Rands ready to give to the guy watching our car. I said that it was cold and windy on the beach. He said it is a nice day today. Sometimes it is so windy that the people don't even get out of their cars. So I suppose we had a lucky day. We did not get blown away.

# Stellenbosch

We already planned by Internet our wine tour by bus for the next morning. Our son had already been to Stellenbosch, which is located in the wine area. He has already slept here in the B&B Banghoek which was cheap and suited more for young people. (http://www.banghoek.co.za),

It was not as good as our other sleeping accommodations, and at first we were disappointed. There were no bathroom tiles and no armoires for the clothes. When taking a shower, all the water landed in front of the toilet on the gray ground. The table on the balcony was so dirty that I had to clean it five times. After we ate some bread, I went downstairs to get a tablecloth for our breakfast the next day. (Why did I not think of that before we ate?) The pictures on the internet looked terrific, nothing like where we were. Perhaps they had built a new part that we did not see.

I thought, how our son could recommend such a terrible place like this? They had a big refrigerator on the ground floor in a big kitchen with tables for eating. After placing my water in the fridge, my leg was black. The refrigerator door was very dirty on the bottom. At night the young people directly under our room had the TV on so loud that I went down there with my pajama on to complain. I put on a jacket naturally.

The nice wine tour the next day allowed us to forget the dismal accommodations. There was a young man who came on the wine trip, and he seemed very lonely. He had visited a friend in the area who now had to work, and the young man was taking his last week of vacation alone. My husband spoke a lot with him because he reminded him of a colleague. The good thing was that this young guy bought some bread on the trip. We bought some cheese and wine but had no bread. *You could not drive to dinner after the wine tasting tour because of the alcohol, so this was our dinner.* Stefan was so nice and offered us half of his bread. He did not want any money for it. He lives in Austria. Another young man on the trip was from London. He was also alone. And there was an older couple from Denmark.

After the wine tour it was still warm and not too late, so my husband and I went into the swimming pool in front of the house. Stefan was reading my little book that I had given him as compensation for the bread. "Ich Versteh Nur Bahnhof – Kurze Geschichten aus dem Leben Einer Deutsch – Amerikanerin".

31

# Crazy Monkeys

We decided to take the route to Mossel Bay through the mountains in the direction of Franschhoek and Route 62, which is a popular and beautiful way to travel back to the coast. It was a cloudy day, but that did not matter, since we were in the car practically the whole day. On the road side we saw some monkeys. They say these monkeys are dangerous and can open your car door! So after taking pictures through the open window, I hurried to close it again. A short time afterwards my husband wanted to get out of the car in order to find some more monkeys. I said you can't get out of the car here! Didn't you hear that these monkeys are dangerous? No way am I going to get out of this car. Who knows where they are?

I was scared and able to convince my husband, that he should not leave the car. We did not see any more of them right away, but later there were some on the road again. Also in other areas we saw some monkeys on the side of the road.

Naturally in Kruger Park there were many of them, and I found their reproduction act interesting and funny. I asked my husband: Did you see that? The male monkey mounted the female for a couple of seconds. Then she walked further. He followed her and repeated the act a couple of seconds more. This procedure was repeated again and again as long as they were in my sight. Others I noticed did the same thing. I asked my husband: Do you know which females are chosen to reproduce? When he said he did not know, I answered, "The ones with the biggest backsides". (I heard that once in a monkey park.)

When we stayed at Kruger Park there were also many different kinds of monkeys. My son said they even open the fridge door, so you should lean a chair against the door. (Our fridge was outside of the cottage there.) You should not have any garbage bags outside because they come around at night looking for food. (At this hut the table, chairs and garbage were all outside.) He was right. As we were safely tucked in our warm beds inside I heard them coming outside. They cry like cats do at night when they are roaming the streets looking for fun. They sound very wild.

# Mossel Bay

Mossel Bay is at the beginning of the beautiful Garden Route. As we drove through the mountains, I saw black clouds ahead and said that we are probably driving toward some bad weather. But luckily the sun was shining as we reached the coast. At the B&B Avenues Guesthouse in Mossel Bay the woman owner was talking to her dog that came out for a walk because apparently he does not like the rain and had hid inside all day. I asked: Was it raining? We did not notice anything besides the dark clouds in the distance, but now the sun is shining. It was already late in the afternoon and she said that they had had a big storm and the electricity was shot off for hours that morning.

The B&B had a swimming pool here too, but it was not warm enough, so we decided to go into the town and look for a good place to eat. She gave us the names of two restaurants, and we drove to the coast.

The town looked like a ghost town. The streets were empty. In the first restaurant on the beach, it stank so much like fish that we both quickly turned around and left. Ok. It is a fish restaurant but it smelled awful. We finally found the second restaurant on the map next to the museum that the women at the B&B gave us.

As I approached the restaurant the first time, I could not open the heavy door and thought they were closed. Luckily the waitress came and opened it. I mentioned that there are no people anywhere, and the waitress told us it was probably because the town had no electricity for hours and many people decided to stay at home. However, she said that we must have brought the sun with us, because now there is no rain.

It was nice, but it was too early to eat, so we went to the bar behind the restaurant and drank a cocktail. They did not have a

"Happy Hour," and when we explained to the bartender what that was, he admitted it would be a good idea. We saw the sun set there and took a lot of nice pictures. There was a pool with one of these machines that all the pools seem to have in South Africa. They move from one end to another. I call it "the monster" when I'm in the pool because I get the feeling that it is going after me all the time. Every pool gets cleaned by the same "monster" machine that stays in the water when you swim. Horrifying.


My tourist book about South Africa said that Mossel Bay has the biggest oil refinery in the world, and that is a why the town is dying. Practically all the shops on the main road were vacant. In such a town you cannot do too much, but they've got a nice beach and a museum. My husband had read something about an old boot mail box in the garden of the Maritime Museum. It has a replica of Bartholomew Diaz's Caravel, the ship in which the famous explorer conquered the African shoreline. We did not know that and thought the museum had pictures. We went there in the morning so that my husband could see this old stone mail box in their garden. We bought some post cards there, because they've got a special stamp and we placed the cards in this famous old stone boot mail box. The lady said it gets emptied every day. To me it looked like it hadn't been emptied for years.

Although in the city there was not too much to do or to see, the museum was worth it, and the park there was also very beautiful. The restaurant next door was also very good. Here we ate delicious beef steaks which are not as expensive as in our country. One good thing about Mossel Bay is that you can get inexpensive rooms before going further on the Garden Route.

Because of the storm, there was damage to our B&B house in Knysna where we had planned to stay the next night. I was surprised that the woman in Mossel Bay got a call from Knysna, but she said they are friends. Somehow the other woman knew we were staying here the night. But that was no problem, since we wanted to stay two nights in Plettenberg Bay. I called the B&B there and told the manager that we would now like to stay two nights, as previously planned. I had changed my mind earlier because it would have cost us a lot of money to pay the advancement in Rands from a bank in Germany. For the one night it would have cost 18 Euros extra. Two nights would have been even more expensive. The owner of the B&B agreed, however, to let us pay upon arrival. Normally he would have insisted on an advanced payment, as would have most of the accommodations which I had chosen. During the off-season, however, they know you can sleep practically anywhere, and they are more accommodating. I heard that all the hotels and guest houses are totally booked during the summer time here on the coast of South Africa. They often have 40 degrees Celsius in Cape Town, but the water of the Atlantic Ocean there is not as warm as the Indian Ocean on the east coast.

We drove further along the highway to Plettenberg Bay. We stopped on the way in Wilderness, which has a beautiful 8 km beach. There was a big hotel directly on the beach, and we drank some coffee there on the balcony. We were the only ones outside because it was cold and windy. It would have been nice to stay in such an expensive hotel on the beach, but we could not afford it.

Then we drove on to Knysna, where we saw only the harbor and drove along the lagoon. There were many shops and restaurants at the harbor. Many tourists were there, mostly from England. Since South Africa used to be a colony of England, many English live there. I recognized their accent when they spoke English. We bought some souvenirs. The lagoon was very big, and there were many boats. There was the Wilderness National Park, the Knysna National

Lake Area, the Featherbed Nature Reserve and Knysna Elephant Park but we did not have enough time to walk around. /We wanted to drive further on to our next destination in Plettenberg Bay. On the way, we drove down a small road through the woods to a place where we could see the elephants from the Knysna Elephant Park behind a fence. The visitors were able to stand directly next to the big animals. But we did not want to pay the entrance fee because we knew we would be going to Kruger Park at the end of the trip and would see many animals there.

What we could not see is the Goukamma Nature Reserve which is a 20.minute drive. There lies a pristine beach of golden sands. Numerous hiking trails along 14 km of protected coast, through adjacent dunes and up the banks of the Goukamma River will keep you happily occupied, but we had no time. Self – catering accommodations are managed by Cape Nature.
(www.capenature.co.za)

Also 15 km from Knysna, directly off the N2 highway, is the Garden of Eden which offers a 1 –km wheelchair- and stroller-friendly wooden boardwalk.

We did leave the highway shortly and drove down the mountain to Nature's Valley. Located at the mouth of the Groot (Big) River, Nature's Valley is punctuated by fynbos-covered cliffs, a massive lagoon, beaches and rugged coastal trails. We did not have much time to walk around and I suppose one can spend days in this area. It is so beautiful. You can stay at different places like the Tranquility Lodge.
(www.tranquilitylodge.co.za)

From June to October is the best time to see the bottlenose dolphins, seals and even whales. The Ocean Blue (www.oceanadventures.co.za) launches open vessels into the surf at Plettenberg Bay. Luckily I found these interesting Websites in Time

Magazine from July9, 2012 on pages 48, 49. If we had more time there then we would have definitely visited all these beautiful places. The whales however do not show up in March.

# Plettenberg Bay

In Plettenberg Bay we had wonderful sleeping accommodations at Gästehaus Pinkepank.
www.urlaub-suedafrika.de
Everything was perfect. We got our city map and a recommendation of where to eat. But on the Internet I had noticed that there is a big, expensive hotel on the coast, the Beacon Island Hotel. That is where I wanted to go for dinner, since we could not afford such an expensive place for the night. My husband was surprised, and I told him that I have already seen the hotel at home on the Internet. The parking lot was directly on the beach, and it looked terrific. There were many rocks and the beach was beautiful.

At each parking lot in South Africa there is always a man with a yellow security vest who watches over the parked cars. I also talked to this man, who told me he always works at night beginning at 6 P.M. because he does not like the sun.

Our first day in South Africa *my son told me that it is sufficient to give these attendants two or three Rands.* You don't have to give them money but they usually wave you out and then you open your window and give him the money, my son told us. Afterwards I always made sure to have some change to give them before I got into the car. My son also shook hands with them and said "how are you?" He told us that *here in Africa, you always ask people first "how are you?" and wait until they say "good thanks and you?" before saying what you really want.* Even if you go to the bathroom, you should say "hello, how are you?" to the cleaning women. The same to the women at the supermarket and to each salesperson you see on the way through the fair. You say it to everyone you meet. I found this very friendly, because the people look each other in the eyes. You give this person your attention and he gives it to you. It shows respect for the other person, even if he is only a cleaning person in the bathroom or a sales person in the supermarket. I thought if they showed this kind of respect in

Germany to all people, then it would be wonderful. But in Germany, people are too absorbed in their own thoughts and hardly notice other people around them. This friendlier behavior in South Africa is something special.

I often talked to the workers at the supermarket and parking lots as well as to many sales people, even if I did not want to buy anything. They all love Germans. They ask where you are from and say, "Germany good." I suppose they have good experiences with Germans, who seem to have a lot of money to spend on vacation. I think we often gave too much of a tip everywhere. For example the taxi driver to the airport in Johannesburg wanted 420 Rands, and we gave 450 Rands. I suppose 30 Rands is a lot of money for them. That is only 3 Euro to us, but they don't earn as much money as the Germans do. My son said that in a restaurant we should leave a 10 percent tip.

We went into the Beacon Island Hotel and found a menu lying on top of some stairs. We looked down and wondered if there was a restaurant in the cellar. The waiter came up and told us to go downstairs. He explained us the 2-menu and 3-menu choices. We decided to have a 2 menu dinner. You practically get the starter for nothing, he told us. I had a beef steak, while my husband had a meat native to South Africa. His meal was good, too, but I preferred the beef steak. I love steaks, and in Africa the food is less expensive than in Germany. My son said they have healthy bulls because they all remain outside and have a lot of space to roam around. We sat in the "basement" at a table directly by a window where the waves where splashing against the orange rocks. There was a light outdoors so that we could see something, because it was already dark outside by 7 p.m. It was very romantic.

The next day we went to the hotel again because the beach in the area was so beautiful. In the morning there was a short period without electricity, but we were lucky to get our breakfast before it happened. We went swimming and got sunburn. It was about 1 p.m., and the sun disappeared behind foggy clouds which reached the water. It was similar to the film "The Fog". You could hardly see two feet in front of you and everything around us seemed to fade away. After a few hours, the sun came back out, but we had already left the beach and drove around. The town was not very big, and we walked down the main street and looked into some shops. My husband thought about buying shoes there, but they did not have his size. He has got big feet. Instead, we ate pizza and then drove to a lookout point over the beach. Then we drove to the other end of town to the Robberg Peninsula.

There is a natural reserve on Robberg Peninsula where you can see whales, dolphins and seals, according to the brochure. Unfortunately it was already very late. The women at the entrance told us the park is open until 8 p.m., and it costs 30 Rands. She explained you need about an hour to walk to the animals from the parking lot. She would have let us in, but it was already half past 6, and if we were not out by 8 p.m. we could get locked in. Plus, the sun was already descending, and in an hour you would not be able to see anything anymore. It would have been stupid to go into the park at such a late hour. I did not want to spend the night there. When it is dark there are no lights anywhere. Even the streets have no lights in the town. I told her that we might come back tomorrow, but after reading in the book that you have to be able to walk very well and that the Robberg Peninsula is no good for people with knee problems, I told my husband, that the excursion there would not be a good idea.

The best thing would be to drive further to our next location in Jeffrey's Bay. That is the surfers' corner. The weather was not so good, and it looked like it would rain, so instead we decided to visit "Monkeyland."
www.monkeyland.co.za

41

There are 11 different types of monkeys there, and we were lucky to see nine of them. We took many pictures, despite the cold. We went on a guided tour with a young girl from Germany who is staying four months in South Africa. She gets her living quarters free but has to pay for her food. I decided to give her 5 Rands as a tip, but did not let my husband know that. He thought the entrance fee was expensive for an hour guided tour, but in fact, it was an hour and twenty minutes.

You can also see different birds directly next to the monkeys, but we did not want to go there.
www.birdsofeden.co.za

We had already seen another young German woman who was spending a half year working at the B&B we stayed at in Cape Town. It seems there are possibilities all over South Africa for young people to work for a while.

On the way to Jeffrey's Bay we drove through Tsitsikamma National Park, which stretches 65 km along the coast. We drove down a steep road to Nature's Valley, where the park begins. We took a short walk there where the lagoon reaches the ocean, but we did not want to take any long walks through the Tsitsikamma Park. We stopped shortly by Bloukrans Bridge, where the highest bungee jump is possible. I wound not want to do such a thing. My son has already jumped and had a back ache for several days afterwards.

Along the way to Jeffrey's Bay we saw some surfers with parachutes jumping high above the waves. It was very windy and perfect weather for them. If we had arrived earlier, we could have observed a school of dolphins that leave the area around 5 p.m. We were half an hour too late. They come in early in the morning and swim outwards again at the same time each day.

# Monster in Pools

As I have already mentioned most pools were oval and all had a cleaning machine that I call "the monster". I first made contact with this movable, blubbering white "monster" at my son's place in Pretoria. I constantly had to watch out not to get caught up in the contraptions's long arm, which is attached to the main energy source. On the floor of the swimming pool this huge round hand sucked its way all over the pool, and I was afraid it would touch my feet. I did not want to be kissed from this "monster" which has a long plastic hose that makes a funny noise as it slowly sucks on the floor and sides of the pool. "Blub,blub,blub".

Practically all pools were oval besides two of them – in Pretoria and Jeffrey's Bay. They had huge normal pools where you can really swim up and down and get some exercise, which is better than just getting wet or cooling off in a pool. Who had this terrible idea that pools should not have any corners anymore?

We swam briefly in most of the pools, which all had this "monster" cleaning the floor. "Can we turn off this thing when we are in the pool?"

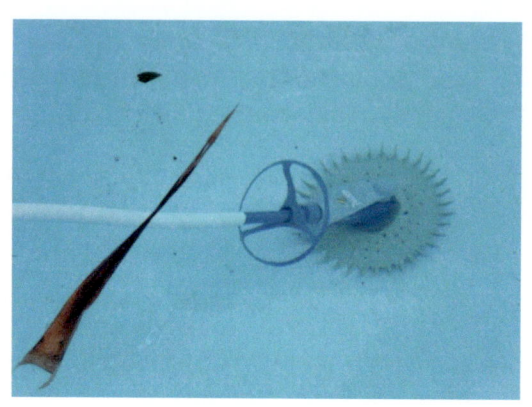

# Jeffrey's Bay

The B&B Ocean Bay in Jeffrey's Bay was very beautiful, and everything looked very new with marble stone and white armoires. Like the other B&Bs that I chose, this one also had German owners, a couple from Munich.

Here are some nice pictures of the hotel and area. http://www.the-ocean-bay.de/

The couple wanted to start something new after they both divorced and decided to move to South Africa. The bed was very big, and most of the beds in Africa that we saw were very high. If you had to get up in the middle of the night to go to the bathroom, you had to watch out that you didn't fall on the ground. They had a big swimming pool with a "sleeping monster," because the pool was too big for the machine. We did not have time then, but the next morning I went swimming there. At least it had four corners and was not oval.

We were hungry and found a good restaurant on the beach where you can eat fish. (This was recommended by the owners of the house where we slept.) Since we had not eaten too much fish yet, we decided to have some. A young man outside by the parking lot said he would watch over our car. He was a young, white guy, and it seemed to me that he was not too smart. How could he earn much money here if only six cars fit into the parking lot? In addition, it is at the end of a street, where it is unlikely for someone to steal a car. But I suppose it is better than not earning any money at all. My husband said that these guys can earn a lot of money working at big parking lots on the beaches. We were told that in Jeffrey's Bay there is not too much of a town to visit and if we want to walk around we should not go further than the police station.

The next day we went into the pool, which was rectangular and not oval. Finally there was a pool in which I could really swim laps. The weather was not so good, and there were clouds in the sky, but it was warm enough. We had enough time because we did not have to drive very far today. We only had 75 km to Port Elizabeth. That was our last destination, and then we would fly back to Johannesburg to our son.

Jeffrey's Bay was small and there was nothing exciting there besides the surfer's beach. I went into the ocean in the afternoon, although I had just taken a shower. My husband walked along the coast looking for sea shells. I quickly noticed that the waves were too big and exhausting for me. When I was a child, I use to dive into the waves on Long Island Beach. There the waves where even bigger than here. But now I am much older and diving into the waves and going under the breaking waves with my nose held closed was exhausting for me. After a few minutes I decided to get out so that the same thing would not happen to me as in Lanzarote. There I lost my balance from the undertow and had to struggle to get out of the water. I was afraid that I might drown there. Here it was not so dangerous, but you can imagine why they call it the surfer's beach.

As we drove around afterward, my stomach became upset. I told my husband I need a bathroom as quickly as possible. We drove through an area where there were poor black people, which made my husband and me nervous. How did we land in such an area? We were actually afraid things might happen that you sometimes hear about. For example it was said that they break through your car window to get to a bag on the back seat. Luckily there was nothing on our back seat. We looked at the town map and concentrated on getting out of there. But actually there was no danger at all. It was only the anticipation that something could happen that made us scared.

We found the main street and drove to the beach, where a famous restaurant was. However, the most important thing for me was the bathroom. The food in Africa can turn your stomach. Both my husband and I had terrible indigestion the past two days. Either we are used to better refrigeration in Germany or we have sensitive stomachs.

# Port Elisabeth

We drove further to Port Elisabeth and almost put the wrong address into the GPS. The same thing happened in Cape Town. Unless you have the name of the suburb, you will end up in the middle of the city. And we were told it can be a dangerous city.

There was a couple we met in Plettenberg Bay and saw later at the airport that told us, they actually drove mistakenly into the city. They had a GPS too, but it did not function correctly at the time. There were only black people in the city, and the few white ones they saw were probably drug attics, they explained. It looked like a very poor area, and they were glad to finally get out of there.

Our host in Jeffrey's Bay had also warned us not to go into the city. He said there was nothing to see there. I thought it was a big city, and my husband also found many things in his tour book to do there. But we were lucky, as our B&B was outside of the city in Summerstrand near the Boardwalk, where everything is secured with guards. **www.africabeach.co.za.**

The Boardwalk is like a small Disney World Park, mostly for children. We walked around, and then went on further to the beach where we ate in a big restaurant on the balcony. On our way back to the B&B, we returned through the boardwalk-complex and went into the casino. They had live music there, and thousands of people were sitting by the slot machines and the betting tables. You could not find a vacant seat anywhere. I noticed that most people were losing money. My husband and I don't want to lose any of our money, so we don't play anywhere.

We just bought something to drink because it was cheap. You needed a membership card, but the man standing there showed his so we could buy something to drink. He was very friendly. He also liked Germans and had been living in South Africa for a long time. After a while, he brought us two new drinks. There are so many friendly people in South Africa.

The next day we spend the morning at the famous beach of Port Elizabeth, which was mentioned in the book my husband had bought about South Africa. We both went swimming there, and the water was very nice. There were very low waves. We were allowed to stay at the B&B until 1 p.m., and I even had enough time to swim shortly in the oval pool with the "monster" before taking a shower.

We had time until 5 p.m. and decided to go to the harbor. Perhaps we misunderstood the couple at Jeffrey's Bay who said the only thing you can do in Port Elisabeth is to eat at the harbor. They probably meant the beach, because we were not allowed to go into the harbor. There were security men who looked into our trunk to see if we had a bomb. We had two big suitcases and I explained we are flying back to Johannesburg today. They told us they are very careful here and look for bombs. Only employees of the harbor are allowed to drive through the gate. We did not know that, and said we did not need to see anything if it is prohibited.

So now we had a few hours time and did not know what to do. We certainly did not want to drive through the city because we heard it is dangerous. Our flight left from the airport at 7 p.m., but we arrived there at 3 p.m. because my husband thought we could spend some time looking around the airport. But there was nothing there to look at. It was very small. And the plane did not arrive on time. Where is it? Still in the air!

We noticed that many planes were delayed, some even for many hours. On the board we could read that our plane will fly at 9:15 p.m. Some other planes were flying to Johannesburg too, and I would have liked to fly with them, but that was not possible.

Then another plane coming from Cape Town got delayed even longer, and now the departure was four hours instead of two hours later. I started to pray that our plane at least will only have a two-hour delay. I heard there is a terrible storm in Cape Town. We were lucky that we had such good weather when we were there.

Our son picked us up from Johannesburg Airport, and the next day we drove toward Kruger Park. It rained practically the whole day, but that did not matter, since most of the time we were on the road. We left North Pretoria where we were staying around 3 p.m. in the afternoon. Our son had already been to Kruger Park and booked a hut for Saturday night. He thought it would be better to spend Friday night outside of the park near the entrance. While driving there, I called some numbers from the book he had about South Africa, but I could not find anything that had a vacancy. It was raining awfully and now and then you could see a car standing on the side of the road, broken down. That must be terrible to be stuck so late in the pouring rain waiting for someone to help you on these long empty roads. We saw lightning with different designs and directions: some horizontal, others vertical. It was surreal.

My husband drove a while so that my son could find a place to sleep for the night. His iPhone has Internet and he looked for a place in some towns, but they all were occupied. He could not believe this. He thought it would be easy to find something for the night. Then he decided to call the number of the farm where he had previously spent the night. We were lucky to find a place for three people. On the way there we bought something for breakfast at a gas station, and shortly before reaching our destination we stopped at Country Fried Chicken and bought a bucket of chicken.

We first had to drive along a long dark road with many pot holes before reaching the gate. Luckily my son remembered how to get there, since there are no lights on the streets and the sign was very small. My son called the owner to tell him we are there so that he would open the gate. Everything is wired with electrical fences to keep out thieves.

For dinner we had three types of chicken and one was very spicy. I didn't eat any of that and found out the next day that my son ate most of them and was having problems. Everything is turning around in his stomach. I know that feeling, I had it already too, I said.

There was thunder and lightning and it was good that we bought something to eat, as we could not have left for a restaurant since it was already 9 p.m. Besides that there were no restaurants in the area. My son told me the next day that he hardly slept because of the noise of the thunderstorm. At some time his fan turned off because the electricity turned off during the night. Our ceiling fan made too much noise and shook too dangerously when you turned it on. To me it looked like it was already one hundred years old, and I was afraid it would fall on me when I am sleeping.

In practically all the rooms we slept in on our journey had a ceiling fan above the bed, and I usually turned it on in the middle of the night when I woke up sweating. I can't imagine how one can sleep in South Africa in the summer when they have hot weather.

My husband was interested in how much they pay for their electricity and had asked a couple of owners. The only thing that was important for me was getting my breakfast. Today we got up at 6 a.m. so that we could be in Kruger Park early. But because there was no electricity, so I could not make any coffee. The toaster also needed electricity. My son and husband were already by the car as the lights and fan turned on. I ran outside and screamed loudly a few times totally excited, the electricity is back. They said I should be quiet, other people are still sleeping. But by the time they came back into the hut, the lights went out again. Oh no, I thought we could have made some coffee. It is terrible if I have to leave the house without having coffee in the morning. The best thing is to sleep in the car.

# Kruger Park

At this site you can get a lot of information about the famous Kruger Park, which is so enormous that you can only see a small part of it. http://www.sanparks.org/parks/kruger/

At 7 A.M. we were already in Kruger Park. My son said you see the most animals early in the morning and in the evening. We all had our cameras ready to take good pictures of many animals. Our goal was to see all the big five, as they are called: elephants, lions, rhinos, leopards and buffalo. We drove to the restaurant to have breakfast. It was too soon to check in, so we drove around with our suitcases until the afternoon. We planned to drive directly to the airport from the park on Sunday. Our flight was at 9 p.m., so we had a lot of time.

It doesn't take long before you start to see the animals. Every time I saw some excrement from a big animal, I knew there had to be some nearby. My son recognized which animals left which excrement, but they constantly walk further, he explained. The best indication of whether there are animals was seeing other cars standing still. Then you watch which direction the people are looking, to the left or to the right. Sometimes the animals were hidden behind some bushes or already out of sight, but other times we were lucky and saw them.

We saw some before checking in and planned a safari tour for the evening. *You have to bring warm clothes because you sit in an open truck.* My son first planned to take two safari tours, but the idea of leaving at six in the morning on Sunday was not a good idea. My husband agreed with me. Besides that, on Sunday my son has to drive us to the airport in Johannesburg and drive back to Pretoria where he is staying for a while.

On the night tour we were lucky and saw four lions. We also saw some nocturnal animals, and it was amazing that the driver saw such small animals. For example we would pass many bushes, and suddenly he would stop and point out a green chameleon sitting on the branch. My husband said that is impossible. They glued an animal here and stop here every night, he joked. There was a small insect we all saw on the street, and I thought it was amazing that he did not drive over it. They provided flashlights so we could point them towards the bushes and see the animals.

I stood up and looked down at the lions walking along the side of the truck. I got scared. I said drive further, because I feared the lion that was looking at me would jump up onto the truck. All the others on the tour were taking pictures and so happy to see these white lions who quickly disappeared behind bushes. Later, when we saw two smaller lions, I wasn't afraid anymore. They disappeared quickly in the dark bushes. The people from the other safari tour were disappointed because they did not see any lions. So we were lucky to get onto the right truck. Some people on the truck wore only shorts or light sweaters. I thought they must be freezing. I had so much on that it became uncomfortable, but the wind was very cold.

My son said we should leave early the next morning, but no one wanted to get up at six o'clock. I said it was good that we did not pay for a morning safari. My son said the summer time is starting now, and we would have missed our tour. That happened to him the last time here too. Daylight savings changed the time by one hour, and he did not know it. Now it is the same time in South Africa as in Germany. But most of the time I was in South Africa, my watch was off by an hour because I do not know how to change the time on it. But my iPhone always had the right time. My son was confused, and I was the only one that got up on time.

I walked over to the kitchen area and cooked some water for the eggs and coffee. We had toast bread but no toaster. We had some cheese but no butter or jelly. At least we had the eggs. My son programmed the airport into the GPS so that we would be able to see what time we would reach the airport any time during our journey. We decided we had time until 1 p.m. to visit more of Kruger Park, and then we should leave the park. It was really good that we did not pay for the early safari; the people we saw on those buses were all freezing, and some were sleeping. It was very cold in the morning on those open trucks, and no one wanted to get up so early in the morning. Besides that, we had to drive to the exit anyway, so we could see the animals ourselves and saved money.

Shortly before the exit we reached our goal of seeing all the five big animals. We finally saw the rhinos, even though they were far away. We only briefly saw the leopard because we got there after he had crossed the street. We saw most of the animals best when they crossed the street. We saw the elephants as they came out of the woods and crossed a narrow river. They came one after another. There must have been at least 50 of them, and they crossed not far from our car. At the end, the biggest came out and stayed a short time with another big elephant. Those must have been the parents. At first I thought they will fight as they got closer to each other by the water, but they actually kissed each other.

We saw a huge number of bulls crossing the street near our car. Giraffes also could be seen and one crossed the street directly in front of our car at the end of the journey. It was good that there were clouds in the sky, because we spend the whole day in the car.

## Sensational Sunsets

We drove a long straight road back to Johannesburg, and on the way stopped at a gas station for some coffee. The restaurants are mostly by the gas stations along the highway. Sometimes you even see bicycle riders on the highway or people standing on the side with their thumb out wanting a ride. Some hold some money in their hand to show they would pay if you take them with you. We had no room because the suitcase was on the back seat, but I would not advise anyone to take a stranger with you, especially in a foreign country.

In the evening the sky was so beautiful and the colors terrific. I constantly took pictures from the car window. When we arrived at the airport, I was sad that we could not watch the beautiful sunset any longer. Especially on the coast of South Africa, we often saw very sensational sunsets, and I took a lot of pictures.

Our son stayed a short time at the airport with us and then left after we had a drink together.

As we walked toward our gate shortly before boarding time, we passed many stores. My husband liked a leather cowboy hat, but we did not have any money. We had given all our Rands to our son and we did not have many Euros either.

Most of the seats at the gate were occupied when we arrived, and we would have had a five-minute wait if they did not mention that there will be a delay because of technical reasons. I said that they should repair what is broken, but the delay was actually because the food was not yet onboard. It took over an hour, and they were still loading the food after we were already onboard. The meals, especially breakfast, are very important to us, so I accepted that necessary delay.

This time I was able to control the screen better to watch the films. I even got a whole row to sit at next to my husband because all the four people sitting in front of the wall got up and changed their seats. So my husband had two seats to sleep on, and I had four but could only put up two armrests. The rest had the tablets and screens in the side. *Don't ever book a seat in a plane directly in front of a wall. There is not very much place for the legs.*

I slept about three hours which was more than on the way there. The sun was shining when we arrived at Munich Airport. We spent a few hours around the airport and took a lot of pictures of airplanes just taking off. It was a wonderful journey. We had wonderful days in South Africa but now are happy to be back in Germany.

Home sweet home.


More "Links" to other books from the author:


http://www.amazon.com/s/ref=nb_sb_noss_1?url=search-alias%3Ddigital-text&field-keywords=Irmgard%20Hetterich


THIS IS A MAN'S WORLD - Isn't it?: I WANT TO KNOW WHAT LOVE IS


http://www.amazon.com/THIS-IS-MANS-WORLD-Isnt-ebook/dp/B00I4F58EQ/ref=pd_rhf_dp_p_d_3


http://www.amazon.de/s/ref=sr_pg_1?rh=i%3Aaps%2Ck%3AIrmgard+Hetterich&keywords=Irmgard+Hetterich&ie=UTF8&qid=1394305078